The Tower Bridge: A Lecture

John Wolfe Barry

A. Joy from the Author
August 1894

THE TOWER BRIDGE.

A LECTURE.

BY

JOHN WOLFE BARRY,

M.Inst.C.E.

London:
BOOT, SON AND CARPENTER,
24, Old Bailey, E.C.

1894.

View of the Tower Bridge in the Spring of 1894.

ERRATA.

Page 43, line 11, for "12 inches" read "27 inches;"

Page 45, line 3, for "their" read "these;"

Page 51, line 16, for "down" read "into."

PREFACE.

THIS Lecture was composed in 1893 for an audience consisting in part of persons well acquainted with engineering matters, but more largely of those who took an interest in the Tower Bridge as members of the general public. It is not to be regarded as being such a professional description of the Bridge as would be suitable to a body of experts; but it may be of interest to a considerable number of persons who have seen the Bridge in its various stages of progress, or who wish to form a general conception of its design and of the various considerations which led up to its inception and determined its mode of execution.

J. W. B.

THE TOWER BRIDGE.

A LECTURE.

BY

JOHN WOLFE BARRY, M.INST.C.E.

Introductory.

BEFORE entering upon a description of the structure of the Tower Bridge, it may be interesting if I touch first upon the history of the principal bridges of London, and then upon the necessity of means being afforded for crossing the river below London Bridge, with a glance at the various suggestions which have been made to meet the want.

A bridge appears to have existed on the site, or a few yards lower down the river than the site, of the present London Bridge, from remote antiquity. We read of Canute attacking and being repulsed from London Bridge, and some writers have held that a bridge at this spot dates from the Roman occupation of London, which was then known to the world as the town Augusta, and must have been of considerable importance. Stow says that in the year 994 the Danes were repulsed in an attack which they made on London, because they took no heed of the bridge; but probably there is some misconception here, for it is recorded that only in the previous year Anlaf, the Dane, sailed up the Thames as far as Staines with ninety-three ships and ravaged the country. Discarding the tradition of a Roman bridge, it seems clear that the first London Bridge of which any record exists was erected between the years 993 and 1016, when Canute attacked London a second time, and made a canal on the south side of the river so as to bring his ships past the bridge. The first bridge was probably of wood, and

FIG 1. OLD PUTNEY BRIDGE.

somewhat of the form which many of us remember in the cases of old Putney and old Battersea bridges, the piers being formed of piles driven into the bed of the river, and the openings spanned by timber beams. (The view (Fig. 1) is taken from a photograph of old Putney Bridge, and illustrates that mode of construction.) This wooden bridge had great vicissitudes. It was washed away in a flood in 1091, was rebuilt in 1097, and burnt in 1136. It was again rebuilt, but was in so bad a state in 1163 that a new bridge was resolved on, and this time in more durable materials.

A certain monk, Peter—Curate of St. Mary, Colechurch—being known for his skill in bridge building, was employed to erect the new bridge, which was begun in 1176 and finished in 1209. Peter of Colechurch did not live to see the completion of his great work, but died in 1202.

The bridge though of stone, gave cause for anxiety early in its history, for the structure was in bad condition in 1280, and five of its arches were borne down by the ice and floods after the great frost of 1282. When the design of the bridge, with its 20 small arches and thick piers, is considered, it will be seen what an obstruction it must have caused to the flow of the water, and how serious the wash must have been through it. In fact, we know that there was, even without any exceptional flood, a fall of five feet on the surface of the water through even the widest of the arches. Apart from the danger to the structure from such a rush of water, the impediment to river traffic must have been very great, and shooting London Bridge in a boat must have been a hazardous enterprise at most times of the tide.

The piers were built on a forest of piles, the tops of which were about 9 feet above the bed of the river; and either originally, or as the necessity for protection to the piles was recognised, starlings or projections all round the piers were added. The starlings consisted of pilework, carried 3 feet above the tops of the main piles of the bridge, the intervening space being filled in with stone or chalk.

The bridge at first was like modern bridges in being unencumbered with houses, except that St. Thomas's Chapel was built on its east side on the ninth pier from the north end. The chapel was 65 feet long, 20 feet wide, and 14 feet high, and it must have projected beyond the roadway on to the pier.

There was a drawbridge near the southern end, partly for defence, but probably also for the passage of ships. To this extent, it was prophetical of the Tower Bridge.

FIG. 2. OLD LONDON BRIDGE.

In 1426 a tower was built on the north side of the drawbridge to resist an enemy, and in 1471 a commencement was made in building houses on the bridge. These were added to from time to time, and amongst them was a famous structure called Nonsuch House, which was a very beautiful building in the architecture of its period, and was greatly admired. I suppose that the houses were chiefly of wood; for it is recorded that, in 1632, forty-two houses were burnt, which were subsequently rebuilt; and, again, in the fire of London in 1666, almost all the houses were burnt, great lamentations being made over their destruction. One would have thought that the bridge was rather improved by the catastrophe: but Londoners did not think so in those days, for it appears to have been an important business street, and the sites were let out to tenants at large rents. In ten years' time the houses were all rebuilt, and the bridge appeared as in the view (Fig. 2) which dates from 1725.

At that time the bridge was described as 915 feet and 1 inch long. Observe the nicety of one inch in such a measurement. Its height above the water was 43 feet 7 inches. The whole width was 73 feet, of which only 20 feet was devoted to the roadway, and 53 feet to the buildings on both sides of it. The approaches to the bridge must have been very steep and inconvenient.

Such was old London Bridge, and so it existed till 1758. It might, I think, be described as inconvenient for road traffic, dangerous for river traffic, and more like an indifferent weir than a bridge over a navigable river. Indeed, its functions as a weir were utilised in 1582; for water wheels were erected in several of the arches at the north end, by which water was pumped for the supply of London.

Whatever we may think now of the ancient bridge, people in the 18th century were proud enough of it, and occasionally burst into poetry about it. Here is a translation, made in 1725, of a Latin ode of the same date in its honour:—

"When Neptune from his billows London spyed,
Brought proudly thither by a high Spring-tide,

As through a floating wood he steered along,
And dancing castles clustered in a throng;
When he beheld a mighty bridge give law
Unto his surges and their fury awe;
When such a shelf of cataracts did roar,
As if the Thames with Nile had changed her shore;
When he such massy walls, such towers, did eye,
Such posts, such irons, upon his back to lye;
When such vast arches he observed, that might
Nineteen Rialtos make for depth and height:
When the Cerulean God these things surveyed,
He shook his trident, and astonished said—
Let the whole earth now all the wonders count,
This bridge of wonders is the paramount!"

There is a little poetical license in more ways than one in the ode; for the Rialto has a span of 90 feet as compared with the narrow openings of old London Bridge, varying from 10 to 30 feet in width and obstructed by the starlings round the piers. You will also see that the local poet was even proud of the cataracts, which endangered the lives of travellers in boats when they shot the bridge with the current, and made it impossible for any one to pass the bridge against the stream.

The houses on London Bridge—or sufficient of them to afford a wide roadway and two good footpaths—were ordered to be finally pulled down in 1746.

Various designs were made from time to time for improving London Bridge, and especially in respect of the waterway. The views (Fig. 3) show two proposals, the upper one by Labeleye, the other by Sir Christopher Wren. Neither design was executed; but that of Wren is a good example of the grasp by that distinguished architect of the problem to be dealt with, and would, if it had been carried out, have been an immense improvement of the navigation.

In 1758-9 an arch 70 feet wide was made (by removing the centre pier of the bridge) for the accommodation of the river traffic: but before long it was felt that the old bridge had outlived its day, and it was replaced by the present beautiful

Fig 3. Labeleye's & Wren's Designs for Improving Old London Bridge.

bridge, by Rennie, which was begun in 1824 and opened in 1831, at a cost, including the approaches, of about £1,500,000. The gradients leading to Rennie's bridge from the south are unfortunately steep, being 1 in 27 from the Borough and 1 in 21 from Tooley Street, and are very distressing to the horses of heavily laden wagons and omnibuses.

It is remarkable how long London existed and flourished with only one bridge across the Thames; for it was not till 1729 that any other bridge was built. This was Putney Bridge, already alluded to, which could, indeed, from its distance from the town, scarcely be called a bridge to serve the needs of London. Such, however, was the jealousy of the Corporation of London that they espied in the project of building a bridge at Putney an attack on the interests of London, petitioned Parliament urgently against it, and prophesied that, if it were authorised, the trade of London would wane and decay.

Putney Bridge cost the modest sum of £23,750, and lasted till 1885, when the handsome stone bridge now existing was built out of the rates, costing, with its approaches, about £600,000. For some years before the bridge was pulled down it had a central opening, which did not exist in the original structure, but was made by removing some of the old piers and spanning the opening by iron girders, supported on iron cylinders.

FIG. 4. OLD WESTMINSTER BRIDGE.

Old Westminster Bridge (Fig. 4) followed soon after Putney

Bridge in order of date, an Act of Parliament having been granted for it in 1735, and the bridge having been opened in 1750. It was 44 feet wide and 1,223 feet long. The centre arch was 76 feet wide, and the whole structure was greatly admired. The cost of it appears to have been about £390,000, which sum perhaps includes the cost of the approaches. The engineer was Charles Labeleye. It fell into decay from failure of the foundations, which rested on timber caissons, and was replaced by the present bridge about 1861. The view is taken from an old print, and gives some idea of the old bridge in its palmy days, before settlements and decay had set in.

Old Blackfriars Bridge (Fig. 5) was authorised in 1750, and opened in 1769. It was not unlike Westminster Bridge and was

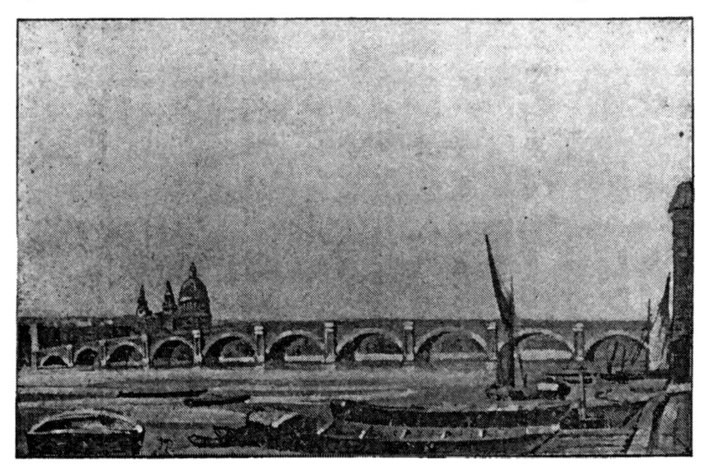

Fig. 5. Old Blackfriars Bridge.

built by Robert Mylne. As in the case of Westminster Bridge, its foundation failed, and from the same causes. It was replaced in 1869 by the present fine bridge, constructed of iron and stone, from the designs of Joseph Cubitt.

It is usual to hear, in these days of iron and steel construction, that the old stone bridges had an element of permanence in them greater than can be hoped for in the case of those constructed of iron or steel. But it is a curious commentary on this view that within our memory Westminster and Blackfriars bridges had to be pulled down within 100 years of their construction, that the piers of Waterloo Bridge have required to be strengthened, and that some of the foundations of new London Bridge have given rise to anxiety.

The main reason of these failures or partial failures is, no doubt, to be found in the increased scour of the river, due to the removal of old London Bridge, which, as has been said, acted very much as a weir, and prevented the free flow of the tide. But it is doubtful whether this was the only cause. Apart from the question of scour, there can be no doubt that stone bridges bring a heavy weight on the foundations, which therefore require great care. They also involve an arched form of construction. The Eastern proverb says truly that the arch never sleeps, and thus defective foundations in an arched bridge involve serious results.

Another bridge of the 18th century was old Battersea Bridge, which was similar to old Putney Bridge.

Vauxhall Bridge was opened in 1816, at a cost of £300,000. It is a poor example of bridge building, and is unworthy of the age which produced Southwark Bridge. It is already found inadequate, and is to be replaced by a better structure.

Waterloo Bridge was designed by Rennie, and was opened in 1817 at a cost of £800,000. It is a very fine work, but is narrower than foresight should have predicted.

Southwark Bridge (Fig. 6), designed by the same engineer as New London and Waterloo Bridges, was, at the time of its erection, and still remains, an excellent example of iron and stone construction. It was opened in 1819 at a cost of

FIG. 6. SOUTHWARK BRIDGE

£800,000, but it also is narrow and the approaches are unduly steep. In the view of Southwark Bridge old London Bridge appears with the central arch as widened in 1759.

Proposals for Crossing the Thames below London Bridge.

We see, from the above imperfect history of bridge building in London during this period, that, though London Bridge alone served our forefathers for upwards of seven centuries, no less than eight bridges were built in a single century, from 1730 to 1830. To this number five more bridges, exclusive of railway bridges, were added in the next half century.

All this activity must have resulted from a great development of South London, and no doubt aided immensely in that development. But London Bridge still remained the bridge lowest down the river, and but little was heard of any other means of crossing the river below this spot till 1824, when Sir Marc Isambard Brunel conceived the project of the Thames Tunnel between Wapping and Rotherhithe.

The difficulties of that work are known to everybody. There were frequent irruptions of water into the works, and it was not till 1843 that the Tunnel was opened for foot traffic only, the original idea of accommodating vehicular traffic having been abandoned, owing to the expense which had already been incurred, and which had amounted to about £468,000. The Thames Tunnel was purchased about twenty-five years ago by the East London Railway Company, whose trains now run through it.

South London, probably, did not begin to extend much below London Bridge till after Lambeth and Southwark had first been developed. I came upon an old print lately (reproduced in Fig. 7) which indicates what Bermondsey was like only 90 years ago. It shows the ruins of the old and famous Abbey of Bermondsey, which stood near the present Tooley Street, and you will see that fields and hedges at that time extended in all directions where now an enormous population lives and labours.

This is merely an instance of what is true of all South London for miles down the river.

It has been stated, I believe correctly, that 39 per cent. of the population of London now live east of London Bridge, and, indeed, a town as large as Manchester and Birmingham put together has rapidly grown up south of the Thames below London Bridge, as is evidenced by any map of London of the present day, which compares strikingly with the print of the

FIG. 7. BERMONDSEY ABBEY.

ruins of Bermondsey Abbey. The question of further communication thus became more and more the subject of discussion, and various attempts (apart from the Thames Tunnel already referred to) were made to deal with the subject, commencing with the Tower Subway.

The Tower Subway, which consists of an iron tube about

7 feet in diameter, extending from Great Tower Hill (on the west side of the Tower of London) to near Pickle Herring Stairs on the Surrey side of the river, was constructed by a joint-stock company, and was opened in 1871, Mr. Peter Barlow being the engineer. It was originally intended to work the traffic through the subway by means of a car drawn by ropes, but, this plan having been found inconvenient, the subway has been since used merely as a footway. In spite of its small size and the inconvenience of its being approached by long flights of stairs, nearly a million foot passengers have passed through it per annum, at a charge of ½d. each.

FIG. 8. METROPOLITAN BOARD OF WORKS PROPOSED TOWER BRIDGE.

In 1879 the Metropolitan Board of Works applied to Parliament for powers to construct a high level, or rather medium level bridge, on the site of the present Tower Bridge. This bridge, designed by the late Sir Joseph Bazalgette, was proposed to consist of a single arch of 850 feet span, supporting a horizontal roadway at a height of 65 feet above high water, and is shown in Fig. 8. It was intended to be approached on the north side by a straight raised approach, rising from opposite the Mint, and on the south side by a long spiral approach, each with a gradient of 1 in 40.

The estimated cost of the bridge was £600,000 for works, £800,000 for property, total £1,400,000, and this expenditure was to have been met out of the rates.

The proposed bridge was strongly opposed by shipowners and wharfingers as being too low, and the long gradients (no less than 5,700 feet in length of 1 in 40) being also thought very objectionable, the scheme was rejected after a long enquiry.

In the Session of 1883 a proposal was made by a private company for a large subway for vehicular traffic, from Great Tower Hill to the Surrey side of the river. Access to this subway would have been afforded exclusively by large and numerous hydraulic lifts. The Bill was opposed by the Metropolitan Board of Works, and was rejected. The subway would not have been toll free.

In 1884 the Metropolitan Board of Works promoted their Thames Crossings Bill, by which they sought to construct a subway for vehicular and foot traffic under the Thames at Nightingale Lane, about a mile east of the Tower. This subway would have been approached by gradients 5,800 feet long of 1 in 40, or somewhat steeper. In the same Session an independent company promoted a "Duplex" bridge at the Tower, on the site of the present Tower Bridge. This bridge, as its name implies, was a double one at the central portion, and its action resembled that of a lock. The down river bridge being opened would allow a vessel to pass up into the space between the two bridges, and when this was done the down river bridge would be closed and the up river bridge opened to allow the vessel to proceed. Of course for vessels descending the river the operation would be reversed. The "Duplex" bridge would have been a great obstruction in the river, and it would have been difficult to manage vessels passing through it with a tide running as it does in the Thames.

The two Bills were referred to a hybrid committee of the House of Commons, who reported that neither Bill ought to be proceeded with, and that a low level opening bridge at the east side of the Tower was the best way of meeting the various opposing views, and they invited the Corporation of London to undertake the work.

Prior to 1884, there had been several proposals for low level bridges at or near the site of the present Tower Bridge—one for example by Colonel Haywood for a fixed bridge without an opening span, others by Sir Douglas Galton and Sir John Hawkshaw for an opening bridge of the ordinary type, with horizontal girders revolving on a central pier. There were also proposals by Sir G. Bruce for a bridge which would roll transversely across the river on isolated piers, and various modifications of Sir Joseph Bazalgette's proposal. Early among these various suggestions was a proposal made by Sir Horace Jones (the City Architect) for a bascule bridge.

I may mention, in passing, that the French word "bascule" means a see-saw, and, as applied to a bridge, means a balanced bridge, which can move up and down. The view (Fig. 9) shows one of the old bascule bridges across a Dutch canal. It will be seen that there are two beams balanced on two upright posts, the inner ends of the beams being attached by chains to a hinged platform across the canal, and the outer ends having counter-balance weights on them. As the outer or landward ends of the beams are lowered, the inner ends are raised and pull up the hinged platform and thus open the bridge for the passage of craft. Numerous examples of similar bridges exist in this and other countries.

The Bridge House Estates Committee of the Corporation of London, who, as representing that body, had given for many

FIG. 9. BASCULE BRIDGE ACROSS A DUTCH CANAL.

years much attention to the subject, appointed in 1884 a deputation to visit the Continent, Newcastle-upon-Tyne, and other places where there were opening bridges of various descriptions, and finally they came to the conclusion to recommend the Corporation to accept the invitation of the hybrid committee of 1884 and promote a Bill for the erection at the Tower site of a "bascule" bridge as the best means of meeting the case.

After the original sketches made by Sir Horace Jones, which are reproduced in the two views (Figs. 10 and 11),

FIG. 10. SIR H. JONES'S DESIGN OF A BASCULE BRIDGE (shut against ships).

FIG. 11. SIR H. JONES'S DESIGN OF A BASCULE BRIDGE (open for ships.)

it was seen that any arched form of construction across the central opening would be very objectionable; as the masts of ships would be in danger of striking the arch unless they were kept exactly in the centre of the span.

Accordingly, various other sketches were made, and this was the condition of affairs when in 1884 I became connected with the undertaking as engineer, Sir Horace Jones being at the same time appointed architect to the work, and we decided that any girders over the central span, when open for the passage of ships, must be horizontal and not arched. The result of these considerations was an amended sketch

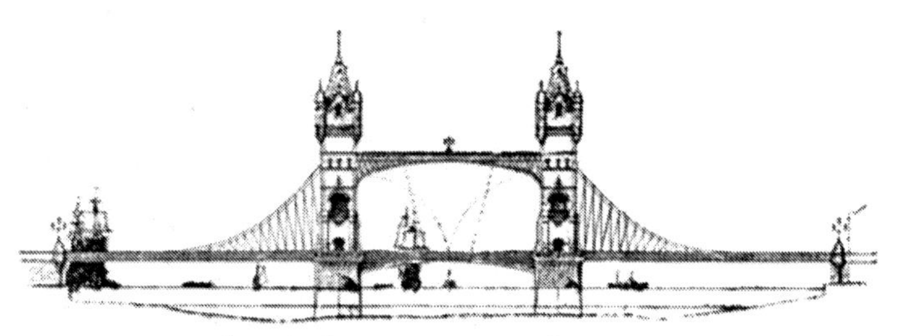

FIG. 12. DESIGN SUBMITTED TO PARLIAMENT.

shown in Fig. 12. In 1885 the Corporation, in accordance with these ideas, promoted the Act of Parliament, of which the present structure, though greatly altered from the original sketch, is the result.

The problem to be solved is one of no small difficulty, for it is necessary to reconcile the requirements of the land traffic with the very important interests of the trade of the Upper Pool. This part of the river is always crowded with craft of various kinds, and this fact made the "bascule" system unusually desirable. Any opening bridge revolving horizontally would have occupied so large an area of the river as to be undesirable from many important points of view, whereas a bridge revolving in a vertical plane, not only occupies the minimum of space in the river, but also at an early stage of the process of opening affords a clear passage for ships in the central part of the waterway, increasing in width rapidly as the operation of opening is continued.

The mode in which the traffic of the Pool is conducted prescribed the general arrangement of the spans of the bridge. Sea-going vessels of all kinds are moored head and stern in two parallel lines in the Upper Pool, on each side of the centre line of the river, leaving a central channel from 200 to 250 feet wide free for the passage of vessels up and down the river, and this space is frequently contracted, by barges and small craft lying alongside the larger vessels, to a width of from 160 to 180 feet. The spaces in the river occupied by the large vessels on each side of the free central channel are called tiers, and as vessels lie in the tiers two or sometimes three abreast, with barges alongside them, it will be seen that if the piers of a bridge were made alignable with the tiers there would be no obstruction to navigation and little to the flow of water by two piers of a width not greater than that of the tiers. On each landward side of the tiers channels are preserved for the passage of vessels to and from the wharves, and it was of course necessary that these side channels should not be obstructed by any pier of the bridge. Thus the mode, in which the river traffic has for many years adjusted itself, made it evident that a bridge with a clear central opening of from 160 to 200 feet, and two side openings of about 280 or 300 feet, would meet all requirements, and that there could be no objection to piers wide enough to accommodate a counter-balance, seeing that the width of two vessels lying in the tiers would be more than the width necessary for such an extension of the moving girders into the piers, as would provide for a sufficient counterpoise.

The proposals of the Corporation, however, encountered a strong opposition in Parliament from the wharfingers, who carried on business with sea-going vessels above the site of the bridge, and the Bill was also opposed by the Board of the Thames Conservancy. The Bill was referred to strong Committees of both Houses of Parliament, and eventually was passed very much in the condition in which it was brought in, but with several stringent clauses for the protection of the interests of the river traffic.

With these few words on the principles that governed the main features of the Tower Bridge, we will proceed to consider the details of the structure generally.

General Description of the Bridge.

The Act of Parliament defined the leading dimensions of the Tower Bridge to be as follows :—

(1) A central opening span of 200 feet clear width, with a height of 135 feet above Trinity high water when open, and a height of 29 feet when closed against vessels with high masts. (It may be mentioned in passing that the height of the centre arch of London Bridge is 29½ feet above Trinity high water.)

(2) The size of the piers to be 185 feet in length and 70 feet in width.

(3) The length of each of the two side spans to be 270 feet in the clear.

The Act also defined the utmost permissible size of the temporary stagings in the river.

The Conservators of the Thames, who very properly considered chiefly the importance of the river traffic, procured the

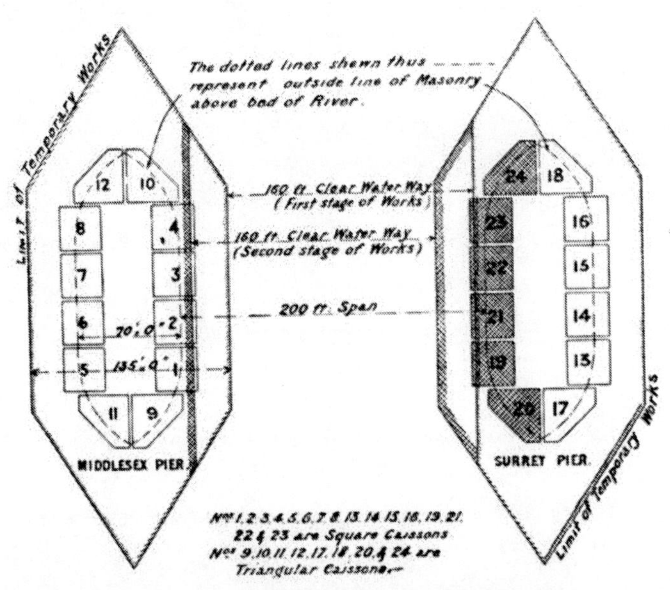

FIG. 13. PLAN TO SHOW LIMIT OF TEMPORARY WORKS.

insertion in the Act of Parliament of a clause obliging the Corporation to maintain at all times during the construction of the bridge, a clear waterway of 160 feet in width, and this necessity occasioned much delay in the construction of the permanent piers, as the opening defined was too wide to permit of both piers being constructed simultaneously. The plan (Fig. 13) shows the limits of the temporary works as defined by Parliament. The outer lines round each pier are the limits of the necessary stagings, and it will be seen that, in order to give a navigable width at all times of 160 feet, there could be only one staging at a time of the full width required for building the piers.

The formal ceremony of commencing the works of the Tower Bridge was performed by the Prince of Wales on 21st June, 1886.

The Government authorities gave every facility for the execution of the works, and, to enable the north approach to the bridge to be made without interfering with very important wharf property, allowed a small part of the Tower Ditch to be occupied by a portion of the works. If this concession had not been made, the cost of the land for the undertaking would have been almost prohibitory. It was stipulated in return that the design of the bridge should be made to accord with the architecture of the Tower, and at one time it was intended that the new works should be made suitable for the mounting of guns and for military occupation. The latter idea was afterwards to a great extent discarded.

The piers of the Tower Bridge are essentially different from the piers of an ordinary bridge, inasmuch as they have to contain the counterpoise and machinery of the opening span, as well as to support the towers which carry the suspension chains of the fixed spans and the overhead girders above the opening span. They are thus very complex structures, as will be seen by the illustrations (Figs. 14, 15 and 16.) Their form in plan (Fig. 15) may be described as a square of 70 feet elongated by cutwaters

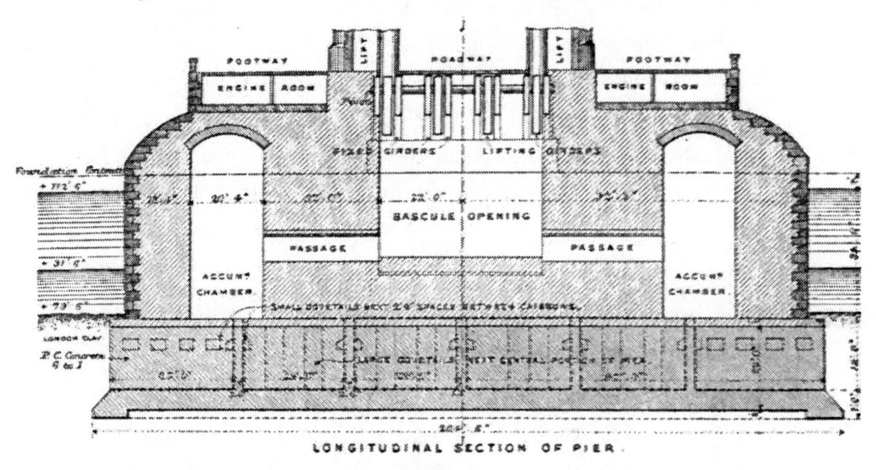

Fig. 14.

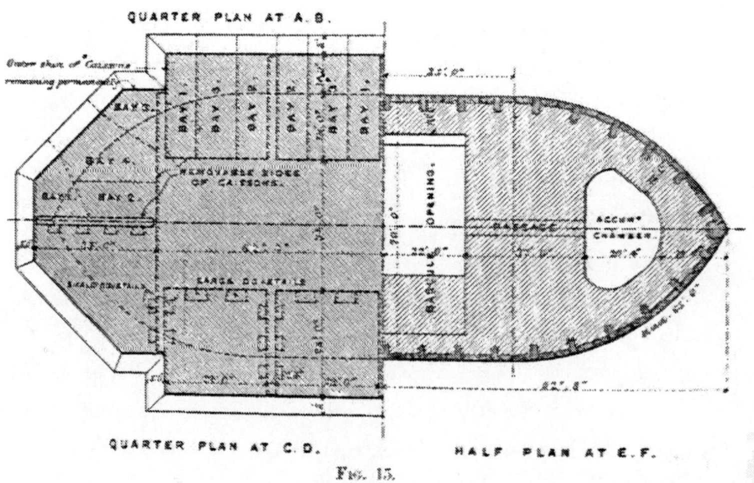

Fig. 15.

at each end, bringing the total length to 185 feet 4 inches. Their total depth from the roadway level to the London clay, on which they rest, is 102 feet.

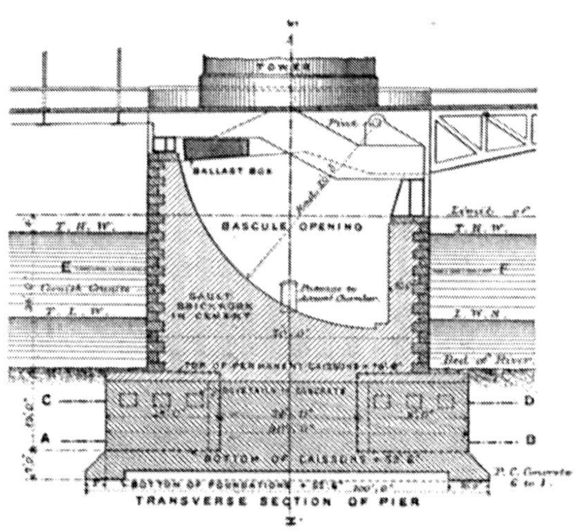

FIG. 16.

We will first consider the form of the piers up to the level of the roadway, which is 32 feet above Trinity high water. Each contains (1) a large cavity to receive the landward end and counterbalance weight of one leaf of the opening span; (2) two large chambers for the hydraulic accumulators; (3) two chambers for the machinery which actuates the opening span; and (4) two long tunnels, one for receiving the main pivot shaft on which the leaf of the opening span revolves, and the other for the pinion shaft by which power is transmitted to the opening span from the machinery.

A diagram (Fig. 28, page 39,) will explain the method of

actuating the opening span. The old bascule bridges of Holland (Fig. 9) had their counterbalance above the roadway level, mounted on posts at the abutments, and attached to the bridge by chains or ropes. The dimensions of the Tower Bridge forbade such an arrangement of an overhead counterweight, and the counterbalance is there applied, as shown in Fig. 28, directly to a prolongation of the girders of the opening span. These girders turn on the main pivot, behind which a space, or cavity, has been provided, to permit of the movement up and down of the landward ends of the girders and the counterweight. This space, which is called the bascule chamber or opening, is in the form of a quadrant, and its dimensions are 50 feet from north to south, 44 feet from east to west ; it is 50 feet in height next the central or opening span, diminishing to nothing next the landward or fixed span of the bridge. The two machinery chambers are each 35 feet by 30 feet, and 10 feet high, and the two chambers for accommodating the accumulators are each 30 feet by 20 feet 4 inches, and are 50 feet in height, extending from below the floor of the machinery chamber to within 26 feet of the bottom of the foundations.

Before describing the mode in which the substructure of the pier was constructed, it will be best shortly to describe the general arrangement of the remainder of the fixed portion of the bridge.

The mode adopted for spanning the landward openings is by suspension chains, which in this case are stiffened. The chains are anchored in the ground at each end of the bridge, and united by horizontal ties across the central opening at a high level (Fig. 30, page 49). These ties are carried by two narrow bridges 10 feet in width, which are available as foot bridges when the bascule span is open for the passage of vessels. The foot bridges are 140 feet above Trinity high water, and, as their supports stand back 15 feet from the face of the piers, their clear span is 230 feet. Access is given to them by hydraulic lifts and by commodious staircases in the towers.

Above the landings, at the tops of the stairs and on which the foot passengers land from the lifts, come the roofs of the towers, the tops of which are 162 feet above the roadway level, or 264 feet from the bottom of the foundations.

Having now given the leading dimensions of the structure, I will proceed to describe (1) the mode in which the piers were constructed up to the roadway level; (2) the details of the opening span and machinery; (3) the details of the fixed superstructure, namely, the towers, the suspension chains, and the overhead footways; (4) the mode of erection of the superstructure.

The Mode of Constructing the Substructure of the Piers.

Iron caissons strutted with strong timbers were used in excavating the bed of the river and building the foundations of the piers. During these operations the external pressure of the water and earth surrounding the caissons was very great, as there is a depth of 32 feet of water at high tide at this part of the river, and the caissons had to be carried about 21 feet into the bed of the river to secure a good foundation. The caissons employed were boxes of wrought iron, without either top or bottom, and with the bottom edges made sharp and strong (Fig. 18,) so as to easily penetrate the ground.

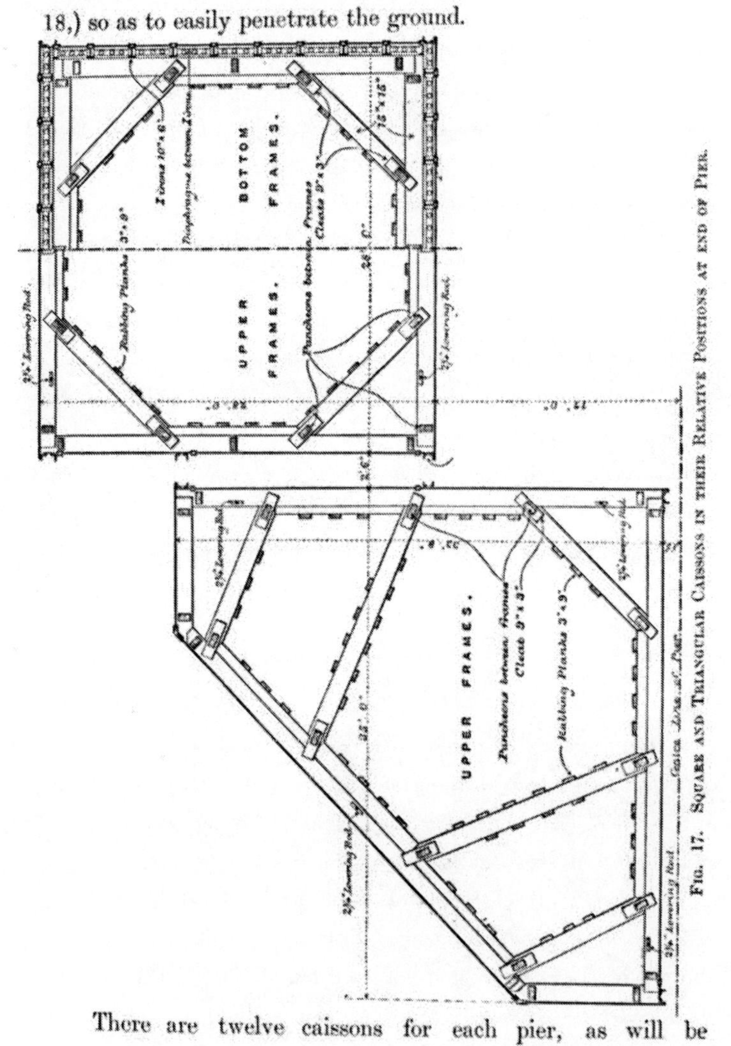

Fig. 17. Square and Triangular Caissons in their Relative Positions at end of Pier.

There are twelve caissons for each pier, as will be

understood from Fig. 13. Those about the central parts of the pier are 28 feet square in plan, and those near the cutwaters are triangular in plan, the dimensions being 35 feet by 33 feet 8 inches. Fig. 17 shows a square caisson and a triangular caisson in plan, with their timbering and other details.

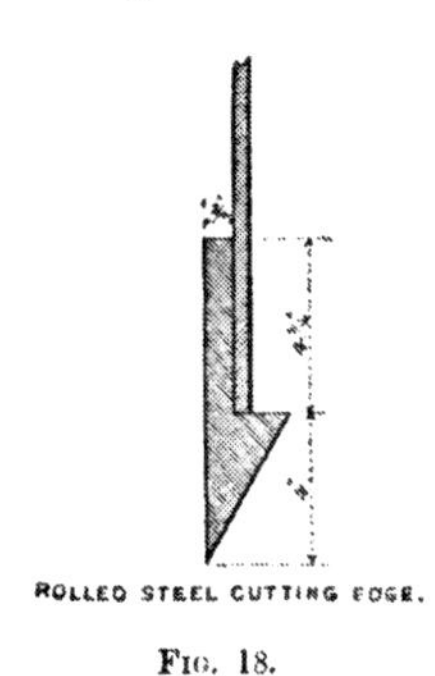

FIG. 18.

I will describe the mode of sinking one caisson, and the description will apply more or less to all, though, of course, the circumstances attending the different caissons required some differences of treatment.

The temporary staging for the pier having been made with piles, the next operation was to erect the caissons upon the staging.

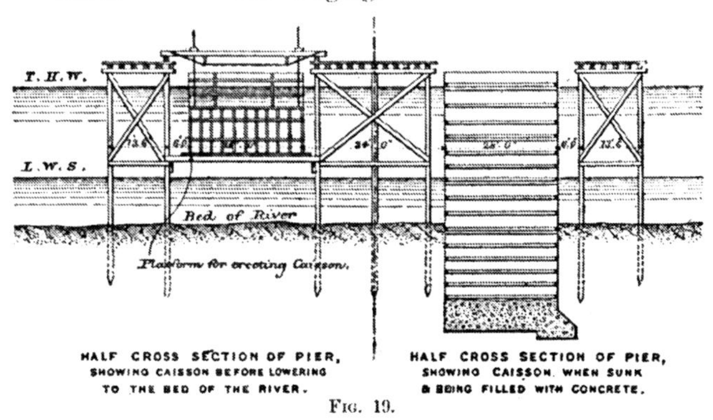

FIG. 19.

The bottom part of the caisson, having to be sunk deep into the bed of the river, could not be removed on the completion of the pier, and was thus named the permanent caisson. The purpose of the upper part of the caisson was merely to exclude the water during the process of building the pier, and it could be removed when the brickwork and masonry were finished. This part was thus called the temporary caisson.

The permanent caisson was 19 feet in height, divided horizontally into two portions. It was erected on timber supports, which were slightly above low water mark (Fig. 19), where it was rivetted together and firmly strutted inside with strong timbers, 14 inches square. It was then lifted slightly by four powerful screws attached to four rods, from which was slung the weight of the caisson and the timbering in it. The timber supports were removed, and the caisson was lowered by the screws on to the bed of the river, which had previously been levelled by divers.

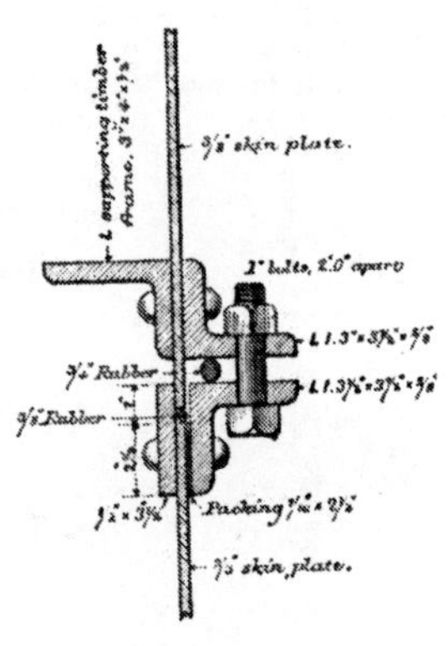

DETAIL OF INDIA-RUBBER JOINT.
FIG. 20.

After the permanent caisson reached the ground various lengths of temporary caisson were added to it till the top of the temporary caisson came above the level of high water. The junction between the permanent and temporary caissons was made with india rubber, as shown in Fig 20.

Divers working inside the caisson, excavated first the gravel and then the upper part of the clay forming the bed of the river, and as they dug away the soil, which was hauled up by a crane and taken away in barges, the caisson gradually sank, until at length its bottom edge penetrated some 5 to 10 feet into the solid London clay.

London clay is a firm, water-tight stratification, and, when the above-mentioned depth was reached, it was safe to pump out the water, which up to this time remained in the caisson, rising and falling with the tide through sluices in the sides. The water having been pumped out, navvies proceeded to the bottom of the caisson and dug out the clay in the dry.

Additional lengths of temporary caisson were added as the caisson sank, so that at last each caisson was a box of iron, 57 feet high and of the dimensions above stated, in which the preparation of the foundations could be commenced. A detailed view of one of the completed caissons is given in Fig. 21.

I may mention in passing how important it is, in order to ensure success in sinking caissons or cylinders, that they should be controlled from above and be prevented from sinking unevenly. It is very easy to prevent a caisson from going wrong (like many animate subjects as well as inanimate) by timely control, but it is a very different thing to put the matter right when a wrong course has been pronouncedly taken.

London clay being peculiarly hard and uniform in texture, advantage was taken of this circumstance to increase the area of the foundations by digging out sideways or undercutting below the edge of the caisson, as shown at the bottom of Fig. 21. The caisson having been controlled from the first by the suspending rods to which allusion has been made, its descent any further than was desired was easily arrested by the rods, when the bottom of the caisson was 20 feet below the bed of the river. The clay was then excavated 7 feet deeper than the bottom of the caisson, and outwards beyond the cutting edge

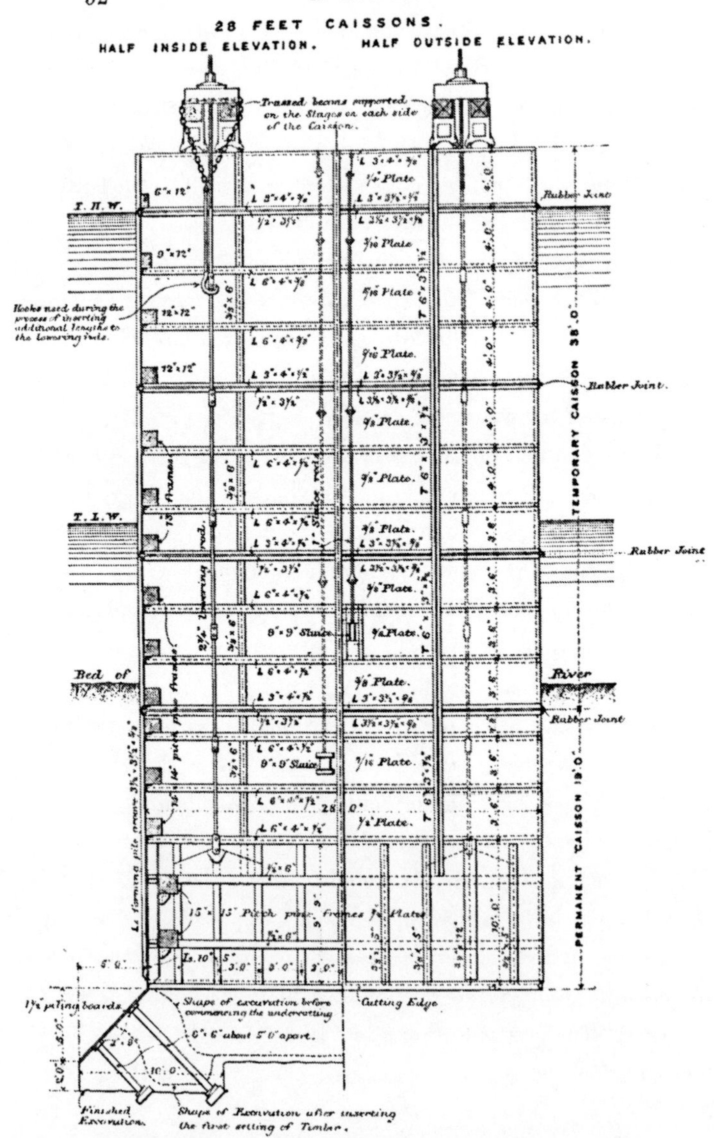

FIG. 21. COMPLETE CAISSON WITH TIMBERING AND SUSPENSION RODS.

for a distance of 5 feet on three of the four sides of the caisson. In this way not only was the area of the foundations of the pier enlarged, but as the sideways excavations adjoined similar excavations from the next caissons (Fig. 22), the whole foundation was made continuous. The whole of the permanent caissons with the spaces between them were then completely filled with concrete, upon which the brickwork and masonry were commenced in the temporary caisson, and carried up to 4 feet above Trinity high water, as shown in Fig. 23.

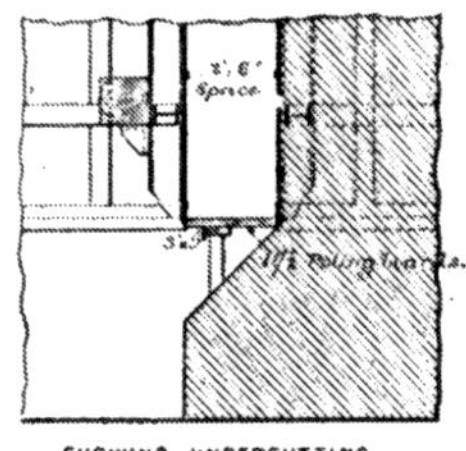

SHOWING UNDERCUTTING BETWEEN TWO ADJOINING CAISSONS.

Fig. 22.

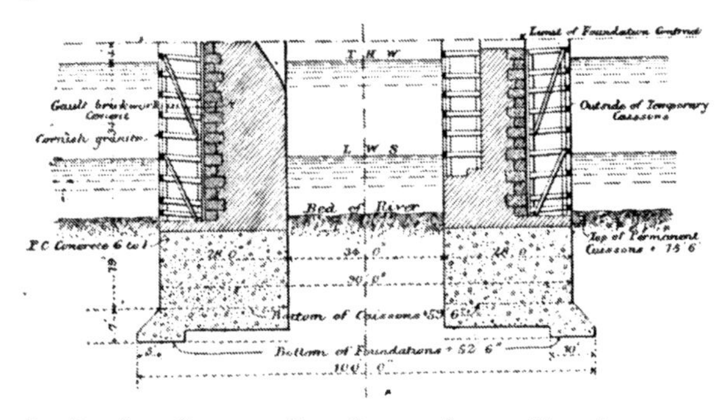

Fig. 23. Cross Section of Pier, Showing Outside Wall Completed.

It was not desirable to build isolated portions of the brickwork and masonry, even if they were joined together afterwards. Accordingly the temporary caissons were so designed as to admit of their sides being removed (Fig. 15) and of the whole area enclosed by their front and back plates being thrown together to permit of continuous building. For this purpose the corners of the caissons were united by timber piles, which were driven in a groove on each caisson (Fig. 24), and when these had been driven and made water-tight (as to which no difficulty

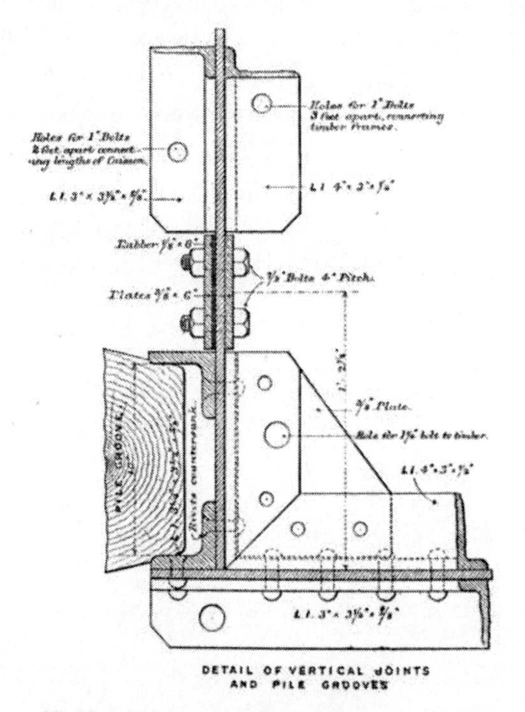

Fig. 24. Enlarged Plan of the Angle of a Caisson.

occurred), the sides of the temporary caissons were removed. In this way the outside portions of the piers were built, and eventually formed a continuous ring of a strong masonry wall, water-tight and able to resist the external pressure of the water. (Fig. 25). The foundations of the central portion of the pier, enclosed by the outside walls, were then excavated and the pier completed.

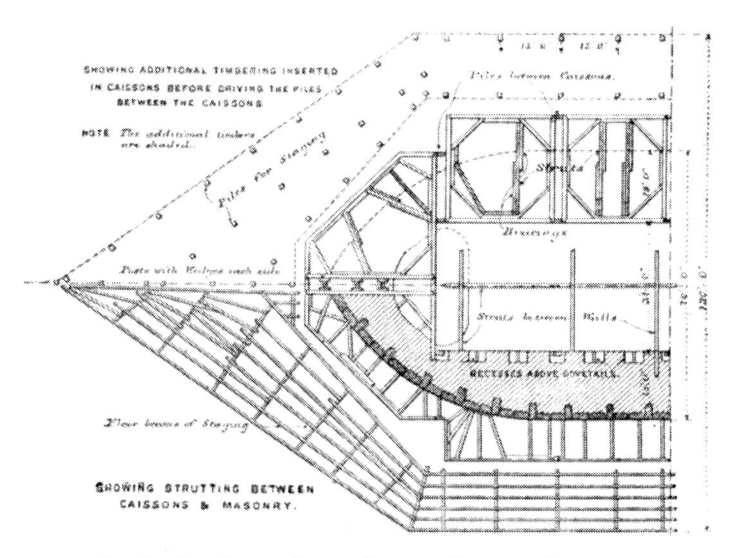

FIG. 25. HALF PLAN OF PIER AT DIFFERENT PERIODS OF CONSTRUCTION.

The abutments of the bridge were built within ordinary coffer dams, and, though formidable in size and depth, presented no new features of construction such as have been explained with regard to the piers.

When the piers and abutments had reached a height of 4 feet above high water, the first contract was finished, and new contracts for the superstructure were let.

The work of the foundations was troublesome and tedious, owing to the isolation of the piers, and still more to the great amount of river traffic, rendering the berthing of barges difficult. The substructure thus occupied a considerably longer time than was anticipated.

FIG. 26. VIEW OF THE FOUNDATIONS IN PROGRESS.

The view Fig. 26 gives an idea of the appearance of the works during the construction of the piers.

The Opening Span.

The stipulated dimensions of the opening span have been already given, as providing, when the bridge is open for ships, a clear waterway of 200 feet in width, with a clear height throughout the 200 feet of 135 feet (which has been increased in construction to 140 feet) from Trinity high water mark. I may mention in passing that I think these dimensions constitute the largest opening span in the world. The next largest opening is, I believe, at the Newcastle bridge, where there are two separate spans of 100 feet each.

The opening span of the Tower Bridge consists, as already explained, of two leaves, each turning on a horizontal pivot of solid forged steel. This pivot, which rests on live rollers, is 1 foot 9 inches in diameter, and weighs 25 tons. Each leaf is formed with four main longitudinal girders, 13 feet 6 inches apart from centre to centre, which together provide for a clear width of bridge between the parapets of 50 feet. This width will be divided into 32 feet for a roadway (which is sufficient for four lines of road traffic) and for two footpaths each 9 feet wide. The spaces between the longitudinal girders are filled with cross girders and roadway plates, on which will be laid the wood pavement of the roadway and footpaths.

The total length of the moving girders resting on each pier is 162 feet 3 inches (Fig. 27). They turn on the main pivot, the position of which is 12 feet 9 inches back from the face of the pier. Thus from the centre of the main pivot riverwards to the end of the girder is 112 feet 9 inches, and to the end of the girders landwards is 49 feet 6 inches. The centre of gravity of the part over the river is 48 feet from the centre of the main pivot, and the estimated weight of this portion of the semi-span is 424 tons. A counterbalance box is attached to the landward end of the girders, and is intended to be filled with 422 tons of iron and lead. The centre of gravity of this portion of the girders and the counterbalance weights will be 32 feet 9 inches from the centre of the main pivot, and the total weight landward of the main pivot will be 621 tons. Thus the total weight of each leaf of the opening span, resting on the main pivot when the bridge is being moved, or on the blocks when the movement is completed, will be the sum of the two weights given above, or 1,045 tons. The pier has, therefore, to carry on its riverward face a heavy load, which is distributed on the masonry by a longitudinal and several cross girders.*

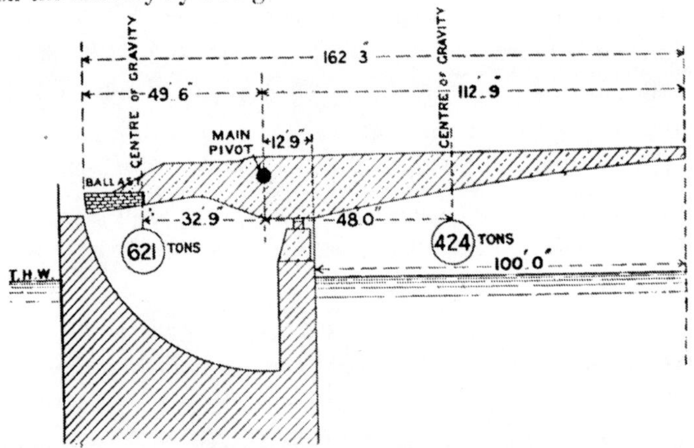

Fig. 27. Diagram of Weights of Bascule.

The two outside girders carry at their counterbalanced ends a quadrant (Fig. 28), on which are fixed teeth, and these teeth engage with similar teeth on revolving pinions, which are actuated by the hydraulic machinery. It will be seen that, when the pinions are turned round, the whole of each leaf of the

* The various weights above given are matters of estimate. They may be slightly modified in execution.

opening span is made to rise or fall at will. It may be mentioned that there are two distinct pinions to each quadrant, making four pinions to each leaf, and that any one of the four pinions is strong enough to actuate and control the whole leaf.

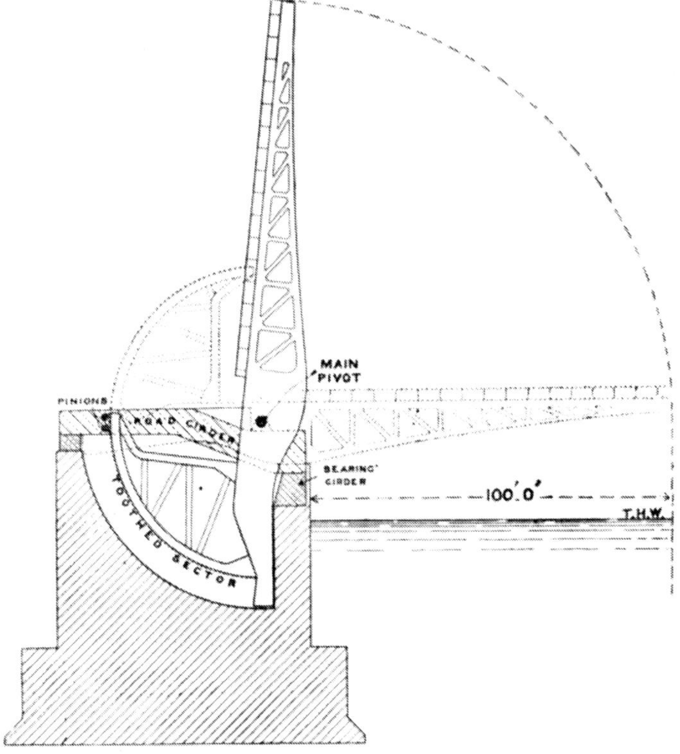

FIG. 28. DIAGRAM OF BASCULE TO SHOW QUADRANT OR SECTOR.

It will be observed that the landward ends of the main girders are bent downwards, and extend backwards into the bascule chamber in the pier, so as to carry the counterbalance box; but it is, of course, necessary that the road and footpaths should extend continuously up to the opening span. This is effected by eight fixed longitudinal roadway girders, which carry the roadway over the bascule chamber, and between which the longitudinal moving girders can rise and fall. Where the moving roadway over the central span adjoins the fixed roadway over the bascule chamber, there must be, of course, a cross slit or joint. This space is covered by a hinged flap, which rises and falls with the movement of the moving girders.

Such are the main features of the opening span, and, before leaving the subject, I will give a short account of the actuating machinery in its main features. It will be, of course, impossible to describe it within the time now available in any minute detail.

Some of my hearers may not be acquainted with the leading principles of hydraulic machinery in general, and so I may be excused if to others my remarks appear somewhat elementary. The principle of the application of water to hydraulic engines is shortly as follows. First of all, a pump is required, which is powerful enough to pump water under great pressure—in the present instance under a pressure of about 850lbs. on every square inch. This pressure is nothing unusual, but its magnitude will be appreciated when we remember that in the boiler of a locomotive engine the steam pressure is usually not more than about one-fifth of the above amount.

The water pressure, being so high per square inch, enables the pistons and pipes of hydraulic machinery to be comparatively small, and, as the water can be conveyed anywhere in pipes of suitable strength, the power produced by the pump can be applied at any desired place. In the present case the pumps are on the Surrey side of the bridge, and are actuated by two steam pumping engines of 360 horse power. The high-pressure water is brought thence by pipes along the Surrey fixed span, up the Surrey tower, across the high level foot bridge, and down the Middlesex tower. Return pipes convey the water—when it has exerted its pressure at the hydraulic engines, which are fixed below the footway on each pier—back again to the pumps at the steam engines, where it is again subjected to pressure and made ready for work again.

There is, however, one important feature of hydraulic machinery to be explained, and that is the accumulator. The object of the accumulator is, as its name suggests, to accumulate power, which is effected as follows. We have seen that the origin of the power is the steam engine actuating a pump or pumps, and, if the machinery were always working and always requiring the same amount of power, an accumulator would be of comparatively little use; for the pumps could pump the water direct to the hydraulic engines, to be used there in a continuous effort. But such is not the requirement. The hydraulic machinery at the Tower Bridge, and in almost every other application of hydraulic power, is not called upon for a continuous effort, but, as it were, for spasmodic efforts lasting over a certain number of minutes, and the accumulators are employed to store up the power provided by the pump, in order to give it out at a greater speed than the pump, though working continuously, would provide.

In accordance with these principles, the accumulator (Fig. 29) is a large cylinder, in which fits a long plunger, on the top of which are placed weights, which bring a pressure of 850lbs. on every square inch of the area of the cylinder. The steam pumps pump water into the accumulator, with that pressure, and

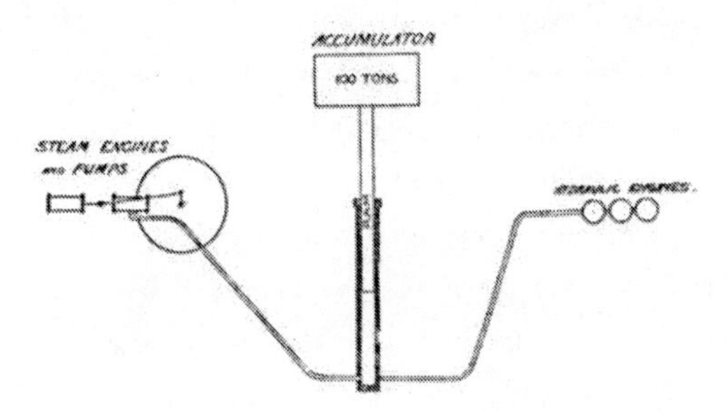

Fig. 29. Diagram of Application of Hydraulic Power.

as it is a principle of hydraulics that any pressure applied to water in a closed vessel is communicated to the whole of the water in that vessel, the pumps, though much smaller than the large plunger of the accumulator, raise it with its superincumbent weight, but proportionately slowly.

The pipes to work the hydraulic engines are in communication with the cylinder of the accumulator, and this, being of great internal capacity, can supply high pressure water with great rapidity to work the hydraulic engines for what I have called their spasmodic efforts. In the meantime, the pumps are working away to re-supply the accumulator.

At the Tower Bridge there are six accumulators, viz., two near the pumps on the Surrey side of the river and two on each pier. Their capacity is ample for the most liberal demands of the hydraulic engines.

It will not be possible to describe the hydraulic engines themselves in any detail. It will be sufficient to say that there are two sets of engines on each pier, and that their leading principle is that of reciprocating cylinder engines. Rams in cylinders are worked to and fro by the high pressure water, and by cranks communicate rotatory motion, through a series of geared wheels, to the toothed pinions, to which allusion has already been made, and which actuate the quadrants of the opening span. Each engine has three rams with a stroke of 12 inches; those on the smaller engines are 7½ inches in diameter, and those on the larger engines 8½ inches in diameter.

When the Tower Bridge was being discussed in Parliament, the disaster to the Tay Bridge was fresh in the minds of many, and some alarm was expressed lest the machinery might not be strong enough to control the opening span in heavy winds. The Board of Trade had reported with regard to the Tay Bridge, that provisions should be made in all future structures for a wind pressure of 56lbs. per square foot, and, though this is, I think, an excessive estimate, even for the wind in such an exposed place as the Firth of Tay, and is much more excessive in the comparatively protected position of the Tower Bridge, it was considered right not only to provide for the extreme pressure of 56lbs. per square foot, but also to provide the machinery of this strength in duplicate on each pier. Thus we have machinery equal to twice the requirements of the Board of Trade. An ordinarily strong wind, however, will not give a pressure exceeding about 17lbs. per square foot, and therefore the hydraulic engines are arranged in pairs, one engine of each pair exerting a power equal to a 17lbs. wind, and the other equal to a 39lbs. wind, the two together being equal to the extravagant pressure of a wind of 56lbs. On each pier the duplicate pair of engines follow up the work of the first pair and provide against breakdowns.

I should mention that when the two leaves of the opening span are brought together, there will be long wedge-shaped bolts, actuated by hydraulic machinery, fixed on one leaf and shooting into the other leaf, to complete the union of the two.

All the machinery of the opening span will be worked from cabins on the piers, in which there will be levers like those in a railway signal box, so interlocked one with the other that all the proper movements must follow in the arranged order.

The time required for the actual movement of the opening span from a position of rest horizontally to a position of rest vertically is estimated at about 1½ minutes. To this must be added the time necessary for stopping the road traffic and clearing the bridge, and withdrawing the bolts. This may take, perhaps, some 1½ minutes more, and we then have to add the time for the passage of a ship and the lowering of the bridge. The time of 1½ minutes for opening or shutting the bridge gives a mean circumferential speed at the extremity of each leaf of 2 feet per second, which is a moderate speed for an opening bridge.

Signals will be provided by semaphores by day and signal lamps by night, to show ships whether the bridge is open or shut. By night when the bridge is open for ships, four green lights will be shown in both directions, and when it is shut against ships four red lights will be similarly exhibited, and their lights will be interlocked with the machinery, so that wrong signals cannot be shown. By day similar intimation will be afforded by semaphore arms on the same posts as those which carry the signal lamps. During foggy weather, a gong will be used in specified ways.

One other part of the machinery remains to be mentioned. This is that of the passenger lifts between the roadway level and the high level foot bridge.

There are two lifts in each tower, consisting of a cage, 13 feet by 6 feet, and 9 feet high, raised and lowered by an ordinary hydraulic ram with chain gearing, and capable of lifting 20 to 25 passengers in about 1½ minutes, including the delays of opening and shutting the doors. As the lift will have to descend carrying a cargo of passengers before it can take a second load of ascending passengers, we may assume three minutes from one start to the next; or, as there are two lifts on each tower, 1½ minutes.

In addition to the lifts, there are ample flights of stairs in the towers.

The Fixed Superstructure.

The fixed parts of the superstructure of the Tower Bridge consist, as has been said, of two shore spans, each of 270 feet, and of a central high level span of 230 feet. The fixed bridge is of the suspension form of construction, and the chains are carried on lofty towers on each pier and on lower towers on each abutment.

I will first describe the towers. When an opening bridge

was first proposed there was some outcry by æsthetical people on the score of its ruining the picturesqueness of the Tower of London by hideous girder erections, and it seemed to be the universal wish that this bridge should be in harmony architecturally with the Tower.

You will have seen the various architectural ideas evolved out of these considerations, and observed that it was originally intended that the towers should be of brickwork in a feudal style of architecture, and the bridge somewhat like the draw-bridge of a Crusader's castle. Subsequently, Sir Horace Jones suggested a combination of brick and stone, and towers of a form similar to that of the view Fig. 12 on page 19.

The ideas were in this condition when I was appointed engineer to the scheme, with Sir Horace Jones as architect, and the Corporation went to Parliament for powers to make the bridge. Sir Horace Jones unfortunately died in 1887, when the foundations had not made much progress, and up to that time none of the architectural designs had proceeded further than such sketches and studies as were barely sufficient to enable an approximate estimate to be made of the cost. Since the death of my coadjutor I have preserved the general architectural features of the Parliamentary sketch designs, but it will be seen that the structure as erected differs largely therefrom, both in treatment and material.

The width, and consequently the weight, of the bridge was increased by the requirements of Parliament, and the span of the central opening was enlarged from 160 feet, as originally intended, to 200 feet. At the same time, the provision of lifts and stairs, to accommodate foot passengers when the bridge was open, was felt to be a necessity.

In this way it became apparent that it would not be possible to support the weight of the bridge on towers wholly of masonry, as in the first designs, unless they were made of great size and unnecessary weight. It was, consequently, necessary that the main supports should be of iron or steel, which could, however, be surrounded by masonry, so as to retain the architectural character of the whole structure.

It was clear that in any event a large part of the steelwork of the towers must be enclosed in some material, for the moving quadrants project upwards some 40 feet from the level of the roadway, while the stairs and lifts also required protection from the weather. It thus became a question of surrounding the towers either with cast iron panelling or with stone, and eventually a granite facing with Portland stone dressings was adopted.

Æsthetically speaking, stone seems better than cast iron, which would equally hide the constructive features, and practically speaking I think it also better, for I know of no mode so satisfactory for preserving iron or steel from corrosion as embedding it in brickwork, concrete or masonry. Careful provision has been made in all parts for expansion and contraction of the two materials, and, though we have had great extremes of heat and cold since the masonry has been built, no effects resulting from any difference of temperature have been observed.

The Fig. 30, which is a half elevation of the steelwork of the bridge, shows the general arrangement of the towers, which have been since enclosed with masonry and brickwork, and may be described as being steel skeletons clothed with stone.

I am afraid some purists will say that the lamp of truth has been sadly neglected in all this, and that the old architects would not have sanctioned such an arrangement as a complex structure of steel surrounded by stone.

One reason may be that the old architects did not know much about iron or steel. Perhaps, if they had been acquainted with their capabilities, they would have been as ready to employ them as they were to back up stone-faced walls with brick, and to hide the constructive features of their buildings as Sir Christopher Wren did when he used a brick cone to support the internal and external domes of St. Paul's.

However all this may be, "needs must when Parliament drives," and, if the appearance of the Tower Bridge is approved, I hope that we may forget that the towers have skeletons as much concealed as that of the human body, of which we do not think when we contemplate examples of manly or feminine beauty.

I return, however, to the details of construction. The skeleton of each tower consists of four wrought steel pillars, octagonal in plan, built up of rivetted plates. The pillars start from wide spreading bases, and extend upwards to the suspension chains, which they support. They are united by horizontal girders and many diagonal bracings, to which it is not necessary here to refer in detail. The chains are carried on the abutments by similar but lower pillars. All these and other particulars appear in Fig. 30.

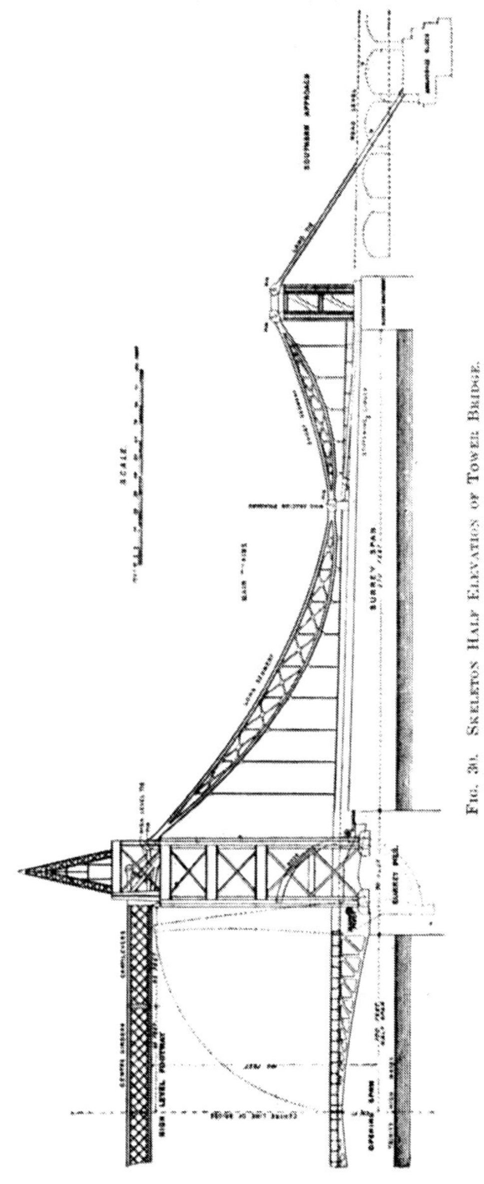

Fig. 30. Skeleton Half Elevation of Tower Bridge.

Between the pillars are spaces for the public stairs and the passenger lifts, and for the quadrants of the opening span when in their upward position. When all these necessary things are accommodated, it will be seen that there is very little room left in the towers for the first 40 feet of their height, that is to say, up to the level of the archway over the road. The horizontal girders in the towers above the archway carry various floors to provide for landings from the public stairs and possibly for rooms for the police and staff.

On the tops of the octagonal pillars rest a series of rollers, which will allow the chains so to move as to accommodate themselves to changes of temperature and to unequal distribution of the road traffic.

The arrangements of the rollers are peculiar. The amount of space available for their reception on the tops of the steel octagonal pillars is limited, while the weight which they have to support is very large, being estimated when the bridge was fully loaded at 1,000 tons. It was thus necessary that the weight should be equally distributed over the whole series of rollers, and that there should be no possibility of a concentration of weight on any one or two rollers. This is effected by an arrangement by which the weight brought on the top of the system is first carried by two blocks, thus ensuring equal division between them, then the weight so divided is sub-divided between two plates, and the weight on each plate is again sub-divided between two rollers.

The main chains, which are 60 feet 6 inches apart from centre to centre, extend from the rollers on the piers to other rollers on each abutment, and support the platform of the bridge by suspension rods, extending from the bottom of the chains to the cross girders of the platform. These arrangements appear in the view, and do not call for any further detailed description.

It may be asked why are these structures, which look like girders, called chains? They are, in fact, chains, stiffened to prevent deflection, and the object of the form is to distribute the local loads due to passing traffic, which, in the case of an ordinary suspension chain, distort the chain, continually depressing each part as the load passes, and consequently distorting the platform of the bridge. By making the chain, as it were, double, and bracing it with iron triangulations, these local deflections of the chain are avoided.

The ends of the chains on the abutments and on the towers are united by large pins to the ties. The ties on the abutments are carried down the ground below the approaches, and are there united to anchorage girders, which rest against very heavy blocks of concrete, and are abundantly adequate to resist the pull of the chains. The ties between the towers are for the purpose of uniting the ends of the two chains, and by their means the stress on the chains is conveyed from anchorage to anchorage.

The platform of the bridge is formed of cross girders, which extend transversely from side to side, their ends being immediately under the chains, to which they are suspended by solid steel rods. Between the cross girders are short longitudinal girders, and on these rest corrugated steel plates, which carry the paving and footways. The total width between the parapets on the fixed spans of the bridge and on the approaches is 60 feet,

FIG. 31. PROGRESS OF TOWER ON PIER IN RIVER.

which is divided into 36 feet for the vehicular traffic and into two pathways each 12 feet wide. I may mention in passing that London Bridge is 54 feet wide between the parapets.

The total weight of steel and iron in the Tower Bridge will amount to nearly 12,000 tons.

The Erection of the Superstructure.

The erection of the superstructure of the bridge has been effected without any considerable difficulty. Temporary stagings of pile work were erected in the river forming piers, upon which wrought iron horizontal girders were erected which supported timber beams and planking thus forming continuous temporary bridges communicating from the shores to each pier. Less difficulty was experienced than was expected in driving the pile work either round the permanent piers or to form the supports of the temporary bridge, and but little damage was ever caused to it during the time of the erection of the bridge by collisions with it of river craft, which from time to time occurred. Access being thus given from the shores, the next thing to be done was to erect the pillars, girders and bracing, forming the steel framework of the abutment and river towers. All the steel work had been put together at the works of Messrs. Sir W. Arrol & Co., at Glasgow, and was brought thence by sea in small pieces to be rivetted together at the bridge. The view (Fig 31) shows this work in progress at one of the river towers.

The next work taken in hand was the erection of the high

level footway bridges between the towers. These bridges when finished are cantilevers for a distance from each tower of 55 feet, and are girders for the remaining space of 120 feet between the ends of the cantilevers. They were erected, however, by

FIG. 32. PROGRESS OF HIGH LEVEL BRIDGES.

temporary expedients, as cantilevers, piece by piece from the tops of the towers and without scaffolding from below, for the whole of the semi-span of 115 feet till they met over the centre of the river. The progress of the girders from week to week as they advanced towards each other, was watched with much interest by the public from London Bridge. A view (Fig. 32) shows the girders a short time before they met.

The chains were erected in their position by means of scaffolds and trestles resting on the temporary bridge. The succeeding views (Figs. 33, 34 and 35) show this work in progress. Cranes on stages, travelling along the temporary

FIG. 33. PROGRESS OF ERECTION OF MAIN CHAINS. SHORT SEGMENT.

wooden bridge, served to place the various parts of the chain on the trestles, where they were rivetted together in their permanent positions. In the meantime the land ties from the anchorages had been brought up to the tops of the abutment towers, and the long horizontal ties, which are carried by the high level bridges, had been erected and rivetted in their places. The holes for the connecting pins at the ends of the ties and at the junctions of the short and long chains were then bored finally and the pins inserted, thus forming a through connection from the

Fig. 34. Progress of Erection of Main Chains. Long Segment.

anchorage on the north side of the river to the corresponding anchorage on the southern side.

Another part of the work was the erection of the fixed roadway girders and the moving girders on the river towers. The fixed girders were first erected on the temporary bridge, and moved from thence into their position over the bascule chamber. The portions of the moving girders which would eventually be landward of the main pivot and extend about 10 feet riverwards therefrom were similarly erected on the temporary

FIG. 35. PROGRESS OF ERECTION OF MAIN CHAINS. GENERAL VIEW.

bridge, launched forward, and placed in a vertical position. The main pivot could now be threaded through the moving girders and the bearings on it adjusted. A sufficient length of the moving girders to reach about 40 feet over the central span of the bridge was then erected vertically, with the accompanying cross girders and bracing, after which the quadrants to carry the teeth by which the moving span was to be actuated, were erected in their places. The teeth of the quadrants were bolted on to them, and, to ensure an accurate fit, with the pinions, which engage with the teeth on the quadrants, the moving girders were revolved by temporary means, so that the teeth on the quadrants could be fitted carefully to those of the pinions. The view (Fig. 36) shows this work in progress. The regulations of the

FIG. 36. MOVING GIRDERS IN PROGRESS.

Act of Parliament rendered it necessary to confine operations in the first instance to a length of 40 feet of the moving girders, so as not to reduce the free passage for vessels through the central opening during the process of adjustment to less than 160 feet. When the adjustment was completed the erection of the remaining portions of the moving girders was taken in hand and the work completed to a height of about 100 feet above the roadway where the ends of the girders are when in their vertical position.

The succeeding view (Fig. 37) shows the general appearance which the bridge will present when opened for the passage of sea-going vessels. It will be observed that the tops of the towers and the ends of the moving girders are incomplete, and

FIG. 37. VIEW OF THE BRIDGE IN THE AUTUMN OF 1893.

that part of the temporary staging in the river, on which the steelwork of the side spans was erected, is still standing.*

I am glad to say that the loss of human life during the construction of the bridge has, considering the magnitude and nature of the works, been small. In all, six men have met with fatal accidents, and at least one of these was the result of sudden illness, or of a fit.

* A more recent view of the Bridge, taken early in 1894, is given as a frontispiece.

The Approaches.

The northern approach to the bridge is constructed partly on a viaduct of brick piers and arches, faced with stone, and partly by means of retaining walls, and extends from the northern abutment to Tower Hill, opposite the Royal Mint, a distance of 330 yards. The ground on which these works stand was acquired from Government, and was the glacis and part of the eastern ditch of the Tower. An entrance to the Tower property from the east is afforded by a wide archway beneath the approach at its southern end. Some of the arches of the viaduct adjoining this entrance are used for a guard room, and others for stores for the fortress and for the bridge. Most of the northern approach is level, and there is a gradient of 1 in 60 on the remainder, extending across the north shore span to the northern pier of the bridge. The southern approach stands wholly on property acquired from private owners, and extends from the southern abutment to Tooley Street, a distance of 280 yards. It is partly constructed on a viaduct near the bridge, and under the arches of the viaduct are placed the engine and boiler houses with the coal stores for the hydraulic pumping engines. The rest of the southern approach is upheld by retaining walls, built so as to form cellarage for houses to be built on each side of the approach. The gradient of the southern approach is, throughout its length, 1 in 40, and this gradient extends across the south shore span to the southern pier of the bridge. From the piers the inclines are continued to the centre of the river by gradients of 1 in 75, on both leaves of the opening span.

Communication between existing thoroughfares and the Tower Bridge.

The approach to the bridge on the north side of the river connects directly with the southern end of the Minories, where that important street, which runs north and south, joins wide thoroughfares extending eastward and westward, but the access from the southern bank of the river is not at present so satisfactory. The approach constructed by the Corporation extends from the bridge to Tooley Street, which is an important street running east and west, but there is no good thoroughfare in a southerly direction from Tooley Street. The London County Council undertook to make a wide southern approach, extending from Tooley Street to the Old Kent Road and Bricklayers' Arms Station; but up to the present time nothing has been done, except to bring into Parliament bills which have been abortive, from the fact that the Council had included in them the principle of what is called betterment. It is much to be hoped that this greatly needed southern approach will be made expeditiously, as it cannot be doubted that, though the heavy traffic of Tooley Street will be served by the present arrangement, much of the utility of the Tower Bridge will remain unrealised, until a direct north and south thoroughfare for traffic is opened up. The Corporation have performed their part of the enterprise, and it is to be regretted that the London County Council are wholly in arrear with their share of the undertaking.

Conclusion.

The accommodation of the interests of the road and river traffic at the site of the Tower Bridge has presented many difficulties, but I venture to hope that the bridge which is now being erected to a great extent solves the problem. Being a low level bridge the total rise of the road traffic is not great, and the gradients of the approaches are short and easy. The river traffic has ample width and height for passing through the bridge, and the machinery for opening the bridge for the passage of ships will be rapid in its action. Lastly, there are arrangements for the continual accommodation of foot traffic.

The seagoing ships which pass the site of the Tower Bridge, and for which the central span would have to be opened, number on the average, about 17 daily. They pass by chiefly at or near the time of high water, and it may well be arranged that several may pass one behind the other. The number of seagoing ships proceeding above the site of the bridge does not show any tendency to growth, but, on the contrary, the volume of such traffic will rather, I think, gravitate to the docks down stream as time goes on.

I am afraid that some disappointment will occasionally be felt when vehicular traffic is stopped by the opening of the bridge, but it may be hoped that no serious delays will occur either to seagoing ships or to vehicular traffic, as the periods during which the opening span will be raised, though sufficient for the accommodation of the river traffic, will not be of frequent occurrence or of long duration. The Tower Bridge will, it is thought, fairly meet all the difficulties of the case, but if the road traffic becomes of greater importance, and the sea-going river traffic grows less, I suppose the fate of the bridge will be to become a fixed bridge. How soon this may happen no one can tell. It is able to fulfil its duties either as an opening or as a fixed bridge.

The cost of the bridge, with its approaches and including the cost of the property purchased, will be about a million sterling, and the whole of the expense will be defrayed out of the funds carefully husbanded and administered by the Bridge House Estates Committee. Londoners will thus be presented, without the charge of one penny on the rates, with a free bridge. The expense of working the bridge, which will be very considerable from the quantity of machinery comprised within it, will also be paid by the Corporation.

As this is the first public authorised notice of the Tower Bridge, I am very glad to take the opportunity of saying how much the works generally, and myself in particular, are indebted to many gentlemen who have assisted in the undertaking. First and most important of all, my acknowledgments are due to my partner, Mr. H. M. Brunel, who has supervised the whole of the complicated calculations and details of the structure, and has taken a very active share in the carrying out of the work from first to last. Afterwards follow the resident engineer, Mr. Cruttwell, who has been in control of the works from their commencement; Mr. Fyson, who has had the duty of the preparation of most of the detailed working drawings and calculations of engineering matters, and Mr. Stevenson, who has acted as my architectural assistant. In connection with this subject, I cannot but express my great regret that the work was so soon after its commencement deprived of the architectural knowledge and experience of Sir Horace Jones, and that he has not lived to see the mode in which his conception of a large bascule bridge across the Thames has been realised. In another branch of duty I have to express my thanks to the various contractors who have been employed—to Mr. Jackson and Mr. Webster, who made the foundations and approaches; to Sir William Arrol to whom the erection of the steelwork of the superstructure is entrusted; to Messrs. Perry, who are carrying out the masonry; lastly, and in a very important degree, to the firm of Sir W. G. Armstrong, Mitchell and Co., to whom is entrusted the hydraulic machinery, which, I believe, is without rival in size and power.

The time of construction, some 7 years to the present time, has seemed long, but it may be some comfort to those who are impatient, to remember that old London Bridge was 33 years in building, old Westminster Bridge 11¾ years, and new London Bridge 7½ years, and I think my hearers will have seen that the Tower Bridge is no ordinary bridge, and in no ordinary position. The structure and its machinery are full of the most elaborate and complicated work of all kinds.

In drawing this description of the works to a conclusion, I may be allowed to express a hope that the Tower Bridge, when finished, will be considered to be not unworthy of the Corporation of the greatest city of ancient or modern times.

6

BOOT, SON AND CARPENTER, PRINTERS, 24, OLD BAILEY, E.C.

CPSIA information can be obtained at www.ICGtesting.com
Printed in the USA
LVOW08s2229070814

398029LV00002BA/402/P